APPLE WATCH S

GENERATION USER GUIDE

A Complete User Manual with Step By Step Instruction For Beginners And Seniors To Learn How To Use The New Apple Watch SE 2ND Gen With WatchOS 9 Tips & Tricks

BY

HERBERT A. CLARK

Table of Contents

INTRODUCTION

Released in September 2022, the Apple Watch SE 2nd generation is the smartwatch for those looking for an affordable, fitness Apple Watch option that features all the key Apple Watch functionalities at a cheap price.

This guide will help you find all the great things the Apple Watch SE 2nd generation can do.

FEATURES OF APPLE WATCH SE 2ND GENERATION

Design & screen

The 2nd-gen Apple Watch SE shares a common design with the original Apple Watch SE, with a slim-bezel display in 40 mm & 44 mm sizes to fit a variety of wrists.

Measuring in at 10.7 mm thick, the Apple Watch SE continues to feature the square design that the Apple Watch has used since its launch in 2015.

All Apple Watch SE are made from 100% 7000 series aluminum, which is lightweight, & affordable. The new smartwatch is available in Midnight, Silver, & Starlight color options.

The Apple Watch SE has 1,000 nits of brightness & Ion-X glass to protect against scratches. The 40mm option has a 324 by 394 pixels resolution, while the 44 mm model has a 368 by 448 resolution.

Battery life

The new smartwatch offers an "all-day" 18-hour battery life from a single charge, which can be increased to about 36 hours with the Low Power Mode.

S8 chip

The new smartwatch has a dual-core S8 SiP, which is the same chip used in the Apple Watch Series 8.

Crash Detection

In the event of a serious car accident, your smartwatch can help you to contact the emergency department & can notify your emergency contacts.

After detecting a serious car accident, your watch will show an alert & start making an emergency call after twenty seconds if you don't cancel it. If you're unresponsive, your watch will play a voice message for the emergency department, informing them that you have been involved in a serious car accident & give them your location details.

Storage space

The new smartwatch has 32 GB of storage space

SETUP YOUR APPLE WATCH

Before you setup your smartwatch, you need to update your iPhone to the newest version of iOS, activate Bluetooth & connect your iPhone to a cellular or WiFi network.

Switch on your smartwatch and wear it

Hold down the side button till you see the Apple symbol on your screen. Then wear your smartwatch on your wrist.

Bring your watch near your iPhone

Wait for the **"Use iPhone to setup Apple Watch"** alert to pop-up on your smartphone, then click on the **Continue** button. If you don't see this message, navigate to the Watch application on your iPhone, click on the **All Watches** button, and then click on the **Add Watch** button.

If this is your personal watch, touch the **Setup For Myself** option.

Ensure your Apple Watch & iPhone are close while you adhere to the directives on your display.

Scan the animation

Set your iPhone in a way that the watch face can be seen clearly in the view finder

If you cannot utilize the camera, or the animation does not appear, or your iPhone cannot scan it, click on the **Pair Manually** button, and then adhere to the directives on your display.

Setup as new or restore from backup

If this is your 1st Apple smartwatch, click on the **Setup as a New Apple Watch** option. If prompted, update your watch to the newest watchOS version.

If you have setup another Apple smartwatch with your current phone, you'll see a screen that says "Make This Your New Watch". Touch App and Data & Settings to see how Express Set up is going to configure your new smartwatch. Then click on the **Continue** button. Click on the **Customize Setting** option if you want to choose how your new smartwatch will be configured. Then select any of the backups from another previous Apple Watch to restore. Or, if you want to completely personalize your smartwatch's settings, click on the **Setup as a New Apple Watch** option.

Select the wrist you want to wear your watch on and then click on **Continue**

Go through the Terms & Condition and then click on **Agree**.

Log in with your Apple ID

If prompted, insert your Apple ID details. If you are not prompted, you can login any time from the Watch application: click on **General**> Apple ID, and then sign in

If the Find My feature is not setup on your phone, you will be prompted to activate the **Activation Lock** feature. If you see the Activation Lock screen, it means your watch has been linked to an Apple ID. You'll need to insert your Apple ID details in the appropriate fields to continue setup.

Create a login code

You can choose to skip this step, but you'll need a passcode if you want to make use of features like Apple Pay.

On your phone, click on the **Create Pass code** or **Add Long Passcode** button, then type your new passcode on your smartwatch. To skip this step, click on **Don't Add Passcode**.

Personalize your settings

Choose your desired size of text.

If you did not make use of Express Set up, your smartwatch will show you the settings it's sharing with your smartphone. If you activate features like Location Services, Diagnostics, Find My, & WiFi Calling for your Phone, these settings automatically activate on your smartwatch.

Setup cellular & Apple Pay

You can setup cellular if your smartwatch is a cellular model.

Next, you will be prompted to configure Apple Pay by adding cards. Then your smartphone will walk you through features such as Always On & your preferred application view.

Allow your devices to synchronize

Your smartwatch will display the watch face when the pairing process has been completed. Keep your smartphone near your smartwatch so that both devices can continue to sync info in the background.

Unpair your smartwatch

❖ Navigate to the Watch application on your smartphone.

❖ Click on the **My Watch** button, then click on the **All Watches** button at the upper part of your screen.

❖ Click on the Information icon ⓘ beside the Apple Watch you want to unpair, and then click on **Unpair Apple Watch**.

APPLE WATCH SE 2ND GEN

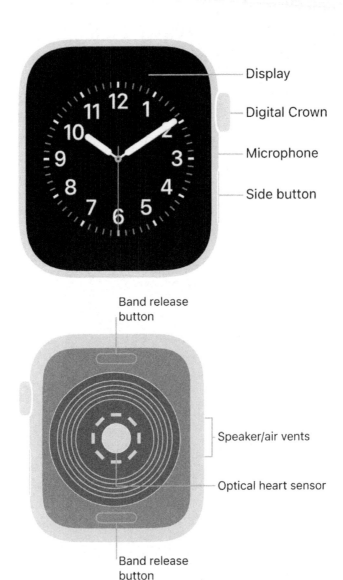

Display

Digital Crown

Microphone

Side button

Band release button

Speaker/air vents

Optical heart sensor

Band release button

WATCH BASICS

Switch your watch on or off

Switch on: Long-press your watch's side button till you see the Apple symbol (you may see a black screen at first).

❖ Switch off: Long-press your watch's side button till you see the sliders, tap the Power button at the upper right, then drag the Power Off slider to the right.

When your smartwatch is off, you can hold down the Digital Crown to check the time.

Tip: You cannot switch off your watch while it is charging. You have to unplug your smartwatch from the charger first before you can turn it off.

Apple Watch gestures

Use the following gestures to interact with your smartwatch.

❖ Tap: Use a finger to touch your watch screen.

❖ Swipe: Move one of your fingers across your watch display.

❖ Drag: Move one of your fingers across your watch display without lifting the finger.

Apple Watch application

With the Watch application on your iPhone, you can change notifications & settings, personalize watch faces, customize the Dock, etc.

Swipe to see your watch face collection.

Settings for Apple Watch.

- ❖ To launch the Watch application, simply touch the Watch application icon on your iPhone.
- ❖ Touch My Watch to check out your Apple Watch's settings.

If you have multiple Apple Watches paired with your iPhone, you'll see the settings for your active smartwatch.

Charge your Apple Watch

- ❖ Put the charger or charging cord on a leveled surface.
- ❖ Connect the charging cable to the adapter.

- ❖ Plug the adapter into a power socket.

❖ Place the Magnetic charger on the back of your watch.

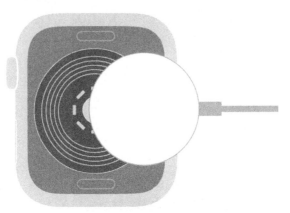

The concave end of the charger will snap to the back of your watch & hold it in place.

Your watch will play a sound when it starts charging and you will see the charging logo⚡ on your watch face

Check the remaining power

To see your watch battery percentage, long-press the bottom of your watch display, then swipe up to reveal the Controls Centre.

Low Power Mode

Activate Low Power Mode to save battery life. Activating this feature will deactivate Always On, background blood oxygen & heartrate measurement. Mobile data will be disabled until when it's needed - for example, when you want to send a message or stream songs.

Note: The Low Power mode will automatically deactivate when your battery is 80% full.

❖ Long-press the bottom of your watch display, then swipe up to reveal the Controls Centre.

❖ Touch the battery percentage, and then activate Low Power Mode.

❖ Scroll down, and touch Turn On Low Power Mode to confirm the choice you've made.
You can touch Turn On For, then select any of the options.

Switch back to normal power mode

❖ Long-press the bottom of your watch display, then swipe up to reveal the Controls Centre.

❖ Touch the battery percentage, and then deactivate Low Power Mode.

Launch applications on your smartwatch

Your smartwatch comes with different applications. To launch an application, simply press the Digital Crown, then touch the application. Press the Digital Crown once more to return to your Watch's Home Screen. You can also download applications from the Apps Store on your watch.

From the watch face, press to see the Home Screen.

Tap to open an app.

Check how long it has been since you last charged your watch

- ❖ Enter the Settings application on your smartwatch.
- ❖ Touch Battery
  You'll see all the information about your watch battery.
- ❖ Touch Battery Health to see the capacity of your smartwatch battery relative to when it was new

Wake your watch

Do any of the below to wake your watch screen:

- ❖ Raise your hand. Your smartwatch will go back to sleep when you put your wrist down.
- ❖ Press the Digital Crown or tap your watch screen
- ❖ Rotate the Digital Crown

Go back to the clock face

You can set how long your smartwatch stays before it goes back to the clock face from an open application.

- ❖ Navigate to the Settings application
- ❖ Head over to General > Return to Clock, then scroll & select when you want your smartwatch to go back to the clock face.
- ❖ You can also press the Digital Crown to go back to the clock face.

Wake up to your last activity

For some applications, you can programme your device to go back to where you were in the application before it went to sleep.

- ❖ Navigate to the Settings application.
- ❖ Head over to General > Return to Clock, then scroll & touch any of the apps, then activate Return to App.

Stop what you are doing in the application to go back to the clock face—for instance, cancel a timer, or stop a podcast.

Keep your smartwatch display On longer

❖ Navigate to the Settings application.
❖ Touch Display and Brightness, touch Wake Duration, and then touch Wake for 70 seconds.

Lock or unlock your smartwatch

Unlock your smartwatch

You can do any of the below to unlock your watch:

❖ Enter your passcode: Wake up your watch, and then type the passcode.
❖ Unlock your smartwatch when you unlock your iPhone: Launch the Watch application on your iPhone, touch the **My Watch** tab, touch Passcode, and then activate Unlock with iPhone.

Your phone & Apple Watch have to be within Bluetooth range (about 33ft) for this feature to work. If Bluetooth is deactivated on your smartwatch, insert the passcode on your smartwatch to unlock it.

Change your passcode

You can follow these steps to change your Apple Watch passcode:

❖ Navigate to the Settings application.
❖ Touch Passcode, touch the **Change Passcode** option, and then adhere to the directives on your display.

Tip: To use a longer passcode, enter the Settings application on your smartwatch, touch the **Passcode** button, and then disable Simple Passcode.

Turn off the passcode

❖ Navigate to the Settings application.
❖ Touch Passcode, then touch Turn Off Passcode

Lock your device automatically

By default, your smartwatch will automatically lock when you aren't wearing it.

❖ To deactivate this feature, enter the Settings application
❖ Touch Passcode, and then disable Wrist Detection.

Lock manually

❖ Long-press the bottom of your display, then swipe up to reveal the Controls Centre.
❖ Touch the Lock button 🔒.

Note: To manually lock your device, you must deactivate the Wrist Detection feature. (Enter the Settings application, touch Passcode, then disable Wrist Detection)

Erase your smartwatch after ten failed passcode entries

Set your device to delete your info after ten failed password attempts

❖ Navigate to the Settings application.
❖ Touch the **Passcode** button, then activate the **Erase Data** feature.

Select a region or language

If you have setup your iPhone to use multiple languages, you can choose the language displayed on your smartwatch.

❖ Enter the Watch application on your phone

❖ Touch the **My Watch** tab, head over to General> Language and Regions, touch Custom, then select one of the languages

Switch wrist or Digital Crown orientation

If you want to start wearing your Apple Watch on your other wrist or would like the Digital Crown on the other side, change your watch settings so that raising your hand will wake your smartwatch, and rotating the Digital Crown will move things the way you expect.

❖ Navigate to the Settings application.
❖ Head over to General>Orientation.

You can also launch the Watch application on your phone, touch the **My Watch** tab, and then head over to General> Watch Orientation.

Remove & replace the bands

❖ Long-press the eject button on the smartwatch.

❖ Slide the band to remove it from your watch, then slide another band in.

Display applications in a list or on a grid

The Home Screen allows you to launch applications on your smartwatch.

The Home Screen can show applications in a list or grid view. Adhere to the directives below to pick one:

❖ From your watch face, press the Digital Crown to enter the Home Screen.
❖ Long-press the Home Screen

❖ Select List View or Grid View

Launch applications from the Home Screen

How to launch an application depends on the view you're using.

❖ Grid View: Touch the app's icon. On the Home Screen, rotate the Digital Crown to launch the application in the middle of the screen.

From the watch face, press to see the Home Screen.

Tap to open an app.

❖ List view: Rotate the Digital Crown, and then touch one of the applications.

Turn the Digital Crown to browse the apps.

Tap to open an app.

To go back to the Home Screen from an application, Press the Digital Crown; press it once more to go to the watch face (or tap the clock icon ⌄ on the Home screen in the Grid view).

Launch an application from the Dock

The Dock provides fast access to the applications you use very often

❖ Press the Side button, and then rotate the Digital Crown to scroll through applications in the Dock.
❖ Touch any of the apps to launch it

Turn the Digital Crown to see more apps. Tap one to open it.

Select the applications that will appear in the Dock

The Dock can display the applications you used recently or your 10 favourite applications.

❖ Display recently used applications: Enter the Settings application, touch Dock, and then touch **Recents**. When you open the Dock you'll see the applications you opened recently.

❖ Display your favourite applications: Enter the Watch application on your iPhone, touch the **My Watch** tab, and touch Dock. Select Favourites, click on the **Edit** button, and then click on the Add icon beside the application you want to see in the Dock. Drag the Reorder icon to rearrange the applications. Touch the **Done** button when you are done.

❖ Remove an application from the Dock: Press the side key to open the Dock, then rotate the Digital Crown to the application you would like to remove from the Dock. Swipe an application to the left, then touch X.

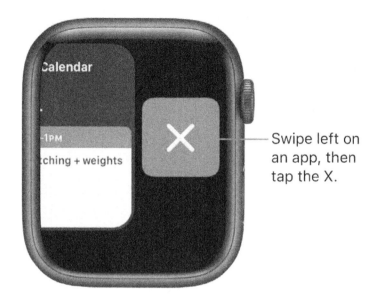

Swipe left on an app, then tap the X.

❖ Go to the Home screen from the Dock: Scroll to the end of the Dock, then click on the **All Apps** button.

Rearrange your applications in grid view

❖ Press the Digital Crown to enter the Home Screen.
❖ Long-press one of the applications, then touch the **Edit App** button.
❖ Drag the application to another location
❖ When you are done, press the digital crown.

Touch and hold an app, then drag to a new location.

Delete an application from your Apple Watch

Long-press the Home screen, touch the **Edit App** button, and then touch X to delete the application from your smartwatch.

In the List view, simply swipe left on the application, then touch the Trash button to delete the application from your smartwatch.

Change the application settings

- ❖ Enter the Watch application on your iPhone.
- ❖ Touch the **My Watch** tab, then scroll to view the applications you've installed
- ❖ Touch one of the apps to make changes to its settings.

View the storage used by applications

You can see how much storage space is being used on your device.

- ❖ Enter the Settings application
- ❖ Head over to General>Storage

Get more applications on your watch

Note: To automatically download the iOS version of an application you have downloaded on your smartwatch, enter the Settings application on your watch, touch Apps Store, and then activate Automatic Download. Ensure you also have Automatic Updates activated to get the latest version of your Watch application.

- ❖ To download applications, enter the Apps Store application  on your watch
- ❖ Rotate the Digital Crown to browse featured applications
  Touch one of the categories or touch the **See All** button under a collection to view more applications.
- ❖ To get a free application, touch the **Get** button. Touch an app's price to buy the application.

  If there's a Download button ⬇ instead of a price, it means you have purchased the application before & you can download it again for free.

Install applications you've already downloaded on your iPhone

By default, applications on your phone that have a watchOS application version are automatically installed & will appear on your watch home screen. If you want to install specific applications only, simply adhere to the directives on your display:

* ❖ Launch the Watch application on your phone
* ❖ Touch the **My Watch** tab, touch the **General** button, then disable Automatic Apps Install
* ❖ Touch the **My Watch** tab, then scroll to the **Available Apps** section.
* ❖ Touch the **Install** button beside the applications you would like to install.

Tell the time on your smartwatch

There're many several ways to tell the time on your smartwatch.

* ❖ Raise your hand: You will see the time when you raise your wrist and look at the screen.

* Hear Time: Enter the Settings application on your smartwatch, touch Clock, then activate the **Speak Time** feature. Place 2 of your fingers on the watch face to hear the time.
  Your smartwatch can also play chimes on the hour. In your Apple Watch's Settings application, touch the **Clock** button & then activate the **Chimes** feature. Touch Sounds to select one of the sound options.
* Feel the time: Your watch can tap out the time on your wrist when it's in silent mode, to activate this feature, navigate to your Watch's Settings application, touch the **Clock** button, touch Taptic Time, activate Taptic Time, then select any of the options.
* Make use of Siri: Lift your hand and say "What time is it?"

Control Center

The Control Centre provides access to Apple Watch features like Flashlight, Theater mode, Focus, etc.

Apple Watch   Apple Watch with Cellular

Touch and hold the bottom, then swipe up to open Control Center.

❖ Open the Controls Centre: Swipe up from the watch face. From any other screen, press & hold the bottom of your watch display, then swipe up.

Note: You cannot open the Controls Centre from your watch's Home Screen. Instead, press the Digital Crown to return to the watch face or launch an application then open the Control Centre.

❖ Press the Digital Crown or swipe down from the upper part of your display to close the Controls Centre.

Rearrange the Controls Centre

❖ Long-press the bottom of your watch's display, then swipe up to reveal the Controls Centre.
❖ Scroll down, then touch the **Edit** button

- Long-press one of the buttons, then drag it to another location.
- Touch the **Done** button when you are done.

Remove the Control Centre buttons

- Long-press the bottom of your watch's display, then swipe up to reveal the Controls Centre.
- Scroll down, then touch the **Edit** button

- Touch the Remove icon  on the edge of the button you plan on removing.

❖ Touch the **Done** button when you are done.

To restore a deleted button, open the Controls Centre, click on the **Edit** button, and then click on the Add icon ⊕ on the edge of the control you would like to add to the Controls Center. Touch the **Done** button when you are done.

Use your smartwatch's flashlight

Use your watch's flashlight to alert other people when you are running in the evening, or illuminate objects near you to preserve your night vision.

❖ Switch on the flashlight: Long-press the bottom of your watch's display, swipe up to reveal the Controls Centre, then touch the Flashlight button ⬖. Swipe to the left to select one of the modes.
❖ Switch off the flashlight: Press the side button or Digital Crown.

Theater mode

This feature stops your watch display from turning on when you raise your hand, so it will remain dark. It also activates silent mode.

Turn theater mode on or off.

Long-press the bottom of your watch's display, swipe up to reveal the Controls Centre, touch the Theater Mode button , then touch Theater Mode

When theater mode is active, the theater status icon  will appear at the upper part of your display.

To wake your smartwatch when Theater mode is active, tap your screen, rotate the Digital Crown, or press the side button.

Activate silent mode

Long-press the bottom of your watch's display, swipe up to reveal the Controls Centre, then touch the Silent Mode button 🔔

Find your iPhone

Your smartwatch can help you locate your iPhone if it isn't far away.

Long-press the bottom of your watch's display, swipe up to reveal the Controls Centre, then touch the Ping button 〔🔲〕

Your phone will make a tone so you can easily find it

Hint: If you are in a dark place, simply Long-press the Ping button & your phone will flash too.

Change Brightness & text size

Enter the Settings application on your smartwatch, then touch Display and Brightness to make adjustments to the following:

❖ Brightness: Touch the Brightness control to make adjustments or touch the slider, then rotate the Digital Crown.
❖ Text size: Touch Text Size, then touch the letters or rotate the Digital Crown.

❖ Bold Text: Activate Bold Text

Change the volume

❖ Enter the Settings application.
❖ Touch Sounds and Haptic.
❖ Touch the volume controls in the Alert Volume section or touch the slider, then rotate the Digital to change the level

Activate or deactivate Digital Crown haptics

You can feel clicks when rotating the Digital Crown to scroll. To activate or deactivate this feature, adhere to the directives below:

❖ Enter the Settings application.
❖ Touch Sounds and Haptic, then activate or deactivate Crown Haptics
  You can also activate or deactivate system haptics.

Use Taptic Time

When your smartwatch is in silent mode, it can tap out the time on your wrist.

- ❖ Enter the Settings application.
- ❖ Touch Clock, scroll down, then touch Taptic Time
- ❖ Activate Taptic Time, then select any of the settings—Morse Code, Terse, or Digits.
  - ➢ Morse Code: Your smartwatch will tap every digit of the time in Morse code
  - ➢ Terse: Your smartwatch will long tap for every 5 hours, short tap for the remaining hours, then long tap for every ¼ hour
  - ➢ Digits: Your smartwatch will long tap for every ten hours, short tap for each hour that follows, long tap for every ten minutes, then short tap for each minute that follows

Respond to notifications when they arrive

Applications can send notifications to keep you informed

- ❖ If you feel or hear an alert, simply raise your hand to check it out.

The notification can either appear as a full-screen notification or in a small banner at the upper part of your screen

❖ Touch the notification to go through it
❖ To clear a notification, simply scroll to the end of the notification, and then touch the **Dismiss** button.

View notifications you have not responded to

If you do not go through a notification when you receive it, it will be stored in the Notifications

Centre. A red dot at the upper part of your watch face indicates that you have unread notifications. To view the notifications, adhere to the directives below:

Swipe down to view unread notifications.

❖ Swipe down from the watch face to open the Notifications Centre. From another screen, long-press the top of your display, then swipe down.

Note: You cannot open the Notifications Centre while viewing the Home screen on your smartwatch. Instead, launch an application or press the Digital crown to enter the watch face.

❖ Swipe down or up or rotate the Digital Crown to scroll through the list of notifications.

❖ Touch one of the notifications to go through it or respond to it.

To delete a message from the Notifications Centre without reading it, swipe left on the notification and then touch tap the **X** button. To delete all notifications, scroll to the top of your display, then touch the **Clear All** button.

Tip: To stop the red dot from appearing on the watch face when you have unread notifications, enter the Settings application, touch Notifications, then disable Notification Indicator.

Mute all notifications on your smartwatch

Long-press the bottom of your watch's display, swipe up to reveal the Controls Centre, then touch the Silent Mode button .

You will still feel a tap when your watch receives a notification. Adhere to the directives below to prevent taps & sound:

❖ Long-press the bottom of your watch's display, then swipe up to reveal the Controls Centre

❖ Click on the DND button 🌙 or the active Focus mode.
❖ Touch the **Do Not Disturb** button, then select any of the available options

Manage your Apple ID settings

You can check out & change the info associated with your Apple ID. You can change your Apple ID password, add & change your contact info, etc.

Change contact info

❖ Enter the Settings application on your smartwatch.
❖ Touch [your name].
❖ Touch E-mail, Phone Number, or Name, then carry out any of the below:
  ➢ Change your name: Touch your name, then touch Last, Middle, or First.
  ➢ View, edit, & add contact info: Touch an e-mail address or number in the **Reachable At** section. To remove an e-mail address, touch it, then touch the **Remove E-mail Address** button.

➤ Add Phone Number or Email Address: Touch the **Add E-mail or Phone Number** button, select Add phone number or E-mail, touch Next, insert the info, then touch the **Done** button.
➤ Hide your e-mail address: Touch Forward To
➤ Change your date of birth: Touch Birthday, then type a new date

Manage your Apple ID passcode & security

❖ Enter the Settings application.
❖ Touch [your name].
❖ Touch Password and Security, then carry out any of the below:
  ➤ Change your Apple ID passcode: Touch the **Change Password** button, and then adhere to the directives on your display.
  ➤ Edit or add a trusted number: Touch your current trusted number, verify when asked to, then touch the **Remove Phone Number** button. To add another trusted number, touch the **Add Trusted Phone Number** button.

> Receive a verification code to log in to another device or iCloud.com: Touch the **Get Verification Code** button.

View & manage subscriptions

❖ Enter the Settings application.
❖ Touch [your name].
❖ Touch the **Subscriptions** button, then touch one of the subscriptions to get more info about it
❖ Touch the **Cancel Subscription** button to cancel & end your subscription

Setup the Handwashing feature on your smartwatch

Your smartwatch can detect when you start washing your hands & encourages you to continue for twenty seconds. Your smartwatch can also alert you if you didn't wash your hands after returning home.

Activate Handwashing

- ❖ Enter the Settings application
- ❖ Touch Handwashing, then activate Handwashing Timer.

  If your smartwatch notices that you have started washing your hands, it will start a twenty-second timer. If you stop washing in less than twenty seconds, it will encourage you to complete your task.

Get handwashing notifications

Your smartwatch can remind you to wash your hands as soon as you get home.

- ❖ Enter the Settings application
- ❖ Touch Handwashing, then activate Handwashing Reminders.

Connect your smartwatch to a WiFi network

- ❖ Long-press the bottom of your watch's display, then swipe up to reveal the Controls Centre
- ❖ Long-press the WiFi button 📶 , then touch the Wifi network from the list.
- ❖ If the network requires a passcode, carry out any of the below:
  - ➢ Touch the Password icon 🔑 , and then select one of the passwords from the list.
  - ➢ Use your iPhone's keyboard to insert the password.
- ❖ Touch the **Join** button.

To forget a network, touch the name of the network, then touch the **Forget This Network** button.

Connect your smartwatch to Bluetooth speakers or headphones

You need to connect to Bluetooth speakers or headphones before you can listen to some audio on your smartwatch. Adhere to the directives that came with the headphones or speakers to set them up. Once your Bluetooth device is ready, adhere to the directives below:

❖ Enter the Settings application, then touch Bluetooth.
❖ Touch the device when it pops up

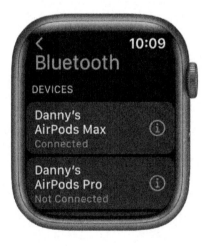 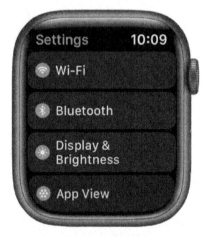

Choose an audio output

❖ Long-press the bottom of your watch's display, then swipe up to reveal the Controls Centre

❖ Touch the Speaker button ⌖ , then select the device you would like to use.

Monitor the volume of the headphones

❖ Long-press the bottom of your watch's display, then swipe up to reveal the Controls Centre

❖ Touch the headphone volume button 👂 while listening to your headphone
A meter will show the current volume of your headphones.

Reduce loud sounds

Your smartwatch can limit your headphone volume to a set decibel level.

❖ Enter the Settings application
❖ Head over to Sounds and Haptics>Headphone Safety, then touch the **Reduce Loud Sound** button

❖ Activate Reduce Loud Sound, then choose any of the decibel levels

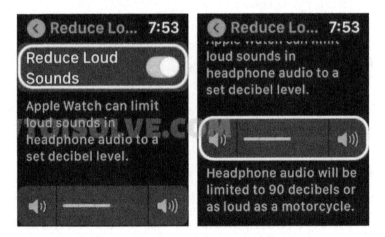

Hand off tasks from you're your smartwatch

The Handoff feature allows you to start a task on one Apple device and finish it on another Apple device. For instance, you can start replying to an email on your smartwatch & finish replying to the email on your iPhone.

❖ Unlock your iPhone
❖ On a Face ID iPhone, swipe up from the lower edge of your display & stop in the middle to reveal the Apps Switcher. (On a Home button iPhone, double-click the Home button to display the Apps Switcher.)
❖ Touch the button that appears in the lower part of the Apps Switcher to continue working in the application

Tip: If you cannot find the button in the Apps Switcher, ensure you have enabled the Handoff on your iPhone in the Settings app> General > AirPlay & Handoff.

To deactivate the Handoff feature on your smartwatch, enter the Watch application on your iPhone, touch the **My Watch** tab, touch General, and then disable the **Enable Hand-off** feature.

Unlock your iPhone with your watch

To allow your smartwatch to unlock your phone when something is preventing Face ID from recognizing your face, simply adhere to the directives below:

❖ Enter the Settings application on your phone, touch Face ID & Passcode, then type your passcode.
❖ Scroll down to the Unlock with Apple Watch section, and activate the feature for your smartwatch.

If you have multiple watches, activate the setting for each of them

❖ To unlock your phone, ensure you are putting on your smartwatch, wake your phone, then stare at the screen.

Your smartwatch will tap your wrist to inform you that your phone has been unlocked.

Note: To unlock your phone, your smartwatch has to have a pass-code, be unlocked, on your wrist, and be near your phone.

Use your watch with a cellular network

With a **GPS + Cellular Apple Watch** & a mobile connection to the carrier used by your iPhone, you can reply to messages, stream podcasts & songs, make calls, etc. on your smartwatch even when you do not have your iPhone or a WiFi connection.

Add your smartwatch to your cellular plan

Adhere to the directives below to activate cellular service:

❖ Enter the Watch application on your phone.
❖ Click on the **My Watch** tab, then click on the **Cellular** button.

Adhere to the guidelines on your display to get more info about your carrier's service plan & activate cellular for your smartwatch.

Activate or deactivate cellular

❖ Open the Controls Center on your smartwatch.

❖ Touch the Cellular button , then enable or disable Cellular.

When your watch is connected to cellular & your phone is not close by, the Cellular button will turn green.

The Cellular button turns green when you have a connection. The green dots show the signal strength.

The green dots show the cellular connection's signal strength.

Check your mobile data usage

❖ Navigate to the Settings application on your smartwatch.

Click on the **Cellular** button, then scroll down to see how much data you have used so far.

Set an alarm

❖ Enter the Alarms application on your smartwatch.
❖ Click on the Add Alarm button.
❖ Touch PM or AM, then touch the Minutes or Hours
This step is not necessary when making use of a 24-hour clock.
❖ Rotate the Digital Crown to make adjustments, then touch the Check icon .
❖ To activate or deactivate the alarm, touch its switch. Or touch the alarm time to set snooze, label & repeat options.

Delete an alarm

❖ Enter the Alarms application on your smartwatch.
❖ Touch the alarm in the Alarms list
❖ Scroll down, then touch the **Delete** button.

Setup your smartwatch as a nightstand watch with an alarm

❖ Navigate to the Settings application on your smartwatch.

❖ Head over to General > Nightstands Mode, and then activate Nightstands mode.

After connecting your smartwatch to its charger with nightstand enabled, it will show the charging status, the date & time, & the time of any alarm you have set. Nudge your smartwatch or touch your screen to check the time.

If you set an alarm, your smartwatch in nightstand mode will gently wake you up.

When you hear the sound, press the side button to turn off the alarm, or press the Digital Crown for Snooze to give yourself some time to rest.

Press to snooze.

Press to turn off alarm.

Calculate on your watch

❖ Navigate to the Calculator application.
❖ Touch the numbers & operators to get answers.

Split the check & calculate a tip

* ❖ Navigate to the Calculator application.
* ❖ Type the total bill, and then touch Tip.
* ❖ Rotate the Digital Crown to select the percentage
* ❖ Touch the **People** button, then rotate the Digital Crown to insert the number of individuals that want to share the bill.

  Next, you'll see the tip amount, the total bill, & how much each person has to pay if the bill is split equally.

Retrace your steps

With the Backtrack feature in the Compass application, you can track your route and then retrace your steps if you get lost.

Note: This feature is used in remote locations, away from the usual places like your workplace or home, and in densely populated places that don't have Wifi.

❖ Enter the Compass application .

❖ Touch the Backtrack icon , and then touch the **Start** button to record your route.

❖ To retrace your steps, click on the "Pause" icon and then click on the **Retrace Steps** button.

The location where you first touched the Backtrack icon will appear on the compass

❖ Follow that route back to go to where you first touched the Backtrack icon.

❖ When you are done, click the Backtrack icon , and then click on the **Delete Steps** button.

Take a screenshot of your watch

❖ On your smartwatch, enter the Settings application, head over to General> Screenshots, and then activate the **Enable Screenshots** feature.

❖ To take a screenshot, press the side button & the Digital Crown simultaneously.

Screenshots are stored in the Photos application on your phone.

Restart your Apple Watch

❖ Switch off your smartwatch: Long-press the Side button till you see the sliders, touch the

Power button , and then slide the Power Off slider to the right.

❖ Switch on your smartwatch: Long-press the side button till you see the Apple symbol

Digital Crown

Side button

Note: You cannot restart your smartwatch when it is charging.

Force restart your smartwatch

If you cannot switch off your smartwatch or the problem persists, you can force restart your smartwatch. Do this if you can't restart your smartwatch.

To force restart your watch, long-press the side button & the Digital Crown simultaneously for about 10 seconds, till you see the Apple symbols.

Erase your watch & settings

❖ Navigate to the Settings application.
❖ Head over to the General > Reset, touch the **Erase All Contents & Setting** button, then type your password.

You can also enter the Watch application on your phone, touch the **My Watch** button, head over to General> Reset, then touch the **Erase All Contents & Setting** button.

If you cannot access the Settings application on your smartwatch because you have forgotten your password, connect your smartwatch to its charger, then long-press the side button till you see the sliders. Long-press the Digital Crown, then touch the **Reset** button.

Backup & restore your Apple Watch

❖ Backup your smartwatch: When connected to your iPhone, content on your Apple Watch is automatically backed up to your iPhone.
❖ Restore your smartwatch from a backup: If you pair your smartwatch to the same iPhone, or buy a new Apple Watch, you can decide to Restore from Back up & choose a saved back up from your phone.

Update your Apple Watch software

You can check for & install software updates.

❖ Enter the Watch application on your phone.
❖ Touch the **My Watch** tab, head over to General > Software Updates, and if there is an update, touch the **Download & Install** button.

Or, enter the Settings application on your smartwatch, then head over to General> Software Updates.

FOCUS

The Focus feature can help you focus when you want to concentrate on a certain task. It can lessen distractions & let other applications & people know that you are busy.

You can select from any of the available Focus modes or create one for yourself on your phone.

Note: If you want to share your Focus settings with all the Apple devices that you're signed in with your Apple ID, navigate to the Settings application on your iPhone, click on the **Focus** button, and then enable **Share Across Devices**.

Activate or deactivate Focus

❖ Long-press the bottom of your watch's display, then swipe up to reveal the Controls Centre
❖ Long-press the current Focus button, then touch one of the Focus modes
  If no Focus mode is active, the Controls Centre will show the DND button 🌙

❖ Select one of the Focus options

To deactivate a Focus, simply touch the Focus button in the Controls Centre.

When Focus is enabled, you will see its icon at the upper part of the watch face, beside the time in applications, & in the Controls Centre.

Create a Focus

❖ Navigate to the Settings application on your iPhone, then touch Focus.
❖ Touch the Add icon, select one of the Focus modes, and then adhere to the directives on your display.

Select a Focus watch face

You can choose a watch face that will be displayed when a Focus mode is activated. For instance, when you activate the Work Focus, your smartwatch can show the Simple watch face.

❖ Navigate to the Settings application on your iPhone, and then touch Focus.
❖ Touch the **Setup** button beside a Focus or create another Focus mode, touch the **Customize Focus** button, then touch Choose under the Apple Watch image

❖ Choose one of the watch faces, then touch the **Done** button.

Create a Focus schedule

You can schedule when each Focus mode occurs on your smartwatch. For instance, you can set the Work Focus mode to activate at 9:30 am and end at 2 pm, from Mondays to Fridays. From 2 pm to 3pm you may have no Focus. Then, activate the Work Focus mode again from 3pm to 6:30 pm, Monday-Thursday.

❖ Enter the Settings application on your smartwatch.
❖ Click on the **Focus** button, touch one of the Focus modes, then touch the **Add New** button.

❖ Touch the From & To options & insert when you would like the Focus mode to activate & deactivate

❖ Scroll down, then select the days you want the Focus mode to be active.
❖ Click on the Return button < in the upper left corner of your display to save the Focus.
❖ Repeat these steps to add more events to the Focus mode.

Deactivate or delete a Focus schedule

To delete or deactivate a Focus schedule, do any of the below:

❖ Deactivate a Focus schedule: Enter the Settings application on your smartwatch, touch the **Focus** button, then touch one of the Focus modes. Touch a schedule, scroll down, then deactivate **Enabled.**
Activate **Enabled** when you want to activate the schedule again.

❖ Delete a Focus schedule: Enter the Settings application on your smartwatch, touch the **Focus** button, then touch one of the Focus modes. Touch a schedule, scroll down, then touch the **Delete** button.

SAFETY FEATURES

Setup & check out your Medical ID on your smartwatch

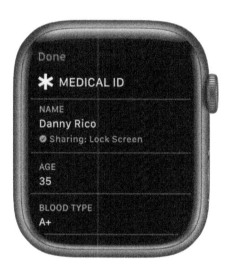

A Medical ID provides your info that may be useful in emergency situations, such as allergies & medical conditions. After setting up your Medical ID in the Health application on your phone, that information is automatically available on your smartwatch. If you share your Medical ID, your smartwatch can send your medical info to emergency services when you contact 911 or use SOS Emergency (US & Canada only).

Your smartwatch can display your medical ID so that emergency personnel can see it.

Adhere to the directives below to view your Medical ID on your smartwatch:

❖ Long-press the side button till you see the sliders.
❖ Drag the Medical ID slider to the right
❖ Touch the **Done** button when you are done.

You can also enter the Settings application on your smartwatch, then head over to SOS> Medical ID.

Contact emergency services with your smartwatch

In an emergency situation, you can use your smartwatch to quickly contact emergency services.

Carry out any of the below:

❖ Long-press your watch's side button till you see the sliders, drag the Emergency Call slider to the right

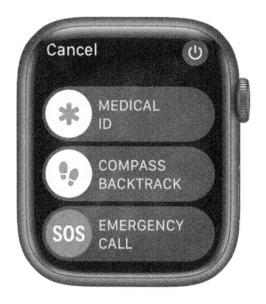

Your smartwatch will contact the emergency services in your area, such as 911 (In some areas, you may need to press a number on the keypad to complete the call.)

❖ Long-press the side button till your smartwatch beeps & begins a countdown. After the countdown, your smartwatch will call emergency services.

If you do not want your smartwatch to automatically start an emergency countdown after long-pressing the side button, simply disable the Automatic Dialing feature. Enter the Settings application on your smartwatch, touch SOS, touch Hold Side Button, then disable the Hold Side Button feature.

- ❖ Say "Hey Siri, call 911."
- ❖ Enter the Messages application on your smartwatch, touch the **New Messages** button, touch the **Add Contacts** button, touch the number pad button, then type 911. Touch the **Create Messages** button, type your message, then touch the **Send** button.

Cancel an emergency call

If you initiate an emergency call by mistake, touch the End Call icon, then touch the **End Call** button to cancel.

Update your emergency address

If the emergency services cannot find you, they'll go to your emergency address.

- ❖ Enter the Settings application on your phone
- ❖ Head over to Phone>Wifi Calling, touch the **Update Emergency Address** button, then insert your Emergency address.

Fall Detection

With Fall Detection activated, your smartwatch can connect you to emergency services & send notifications to your emergency contact if it detects a serious fall. If your watch detects a hard fall & you haven't moved for a minute, it will tap your wrist, play a sound, and try to contact emergency services.

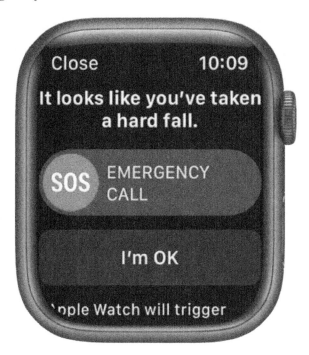

If the date of birth you entered when you setup your smartwatch (or added in the Health application on your phone) indicates that you are fifty-five years or older, the Fall Detection feature is automatically activated. If you are between the ages of 18 & 55, you can enable Fall Detection manually by adhering to the guidelines below:

❖ Navigate to the Settings application on your smartwatch.
❖ Head over to SOS > Fall Detection, then enable Fall Detection.

You can also enter the Watch application on your phone, touch the **My Watch** tab, touch Emergency SOS, then enable the **Fall Detection** feature.

Note: If you deactivate the Wrist Detection feature, your watch would not automatically try to contact the emergency department even if it detects a hard fall.

- ❖ Select the "**Always on**" option if you want Fall Detection to be active all the time or the "Only on during workout" option if you want Fall Detection to only activate when you're working out.

Crash Detection

In the event of a serious car accident, your smartwatch can help you to contact the emergency department & can notify your emergency contacts.

After detecting a serious car accident, your watch will show an alert & start making an emergency call after twenty seconds if you don't cancel it. If you're unresponsive, your watch will play a voice message for the emergency department, informing them that you have been involved in a serious car accident & give them your location details.

Your smartwatch or iPhone has to be connected to a cellular connection before you can call the emergency department.

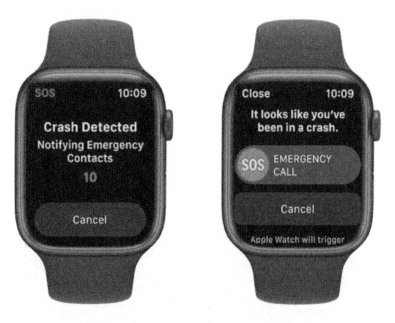

Activate or deactivate Crash Detection

The Crash Detection feature is activated by default. You can disable this feature by adhering to the directives below:

- ❖ Navigate to the Settings application on your smartwatch.
- ❖ Head over to SOS > Crash Detection, then deactivate the **Call after Severe Crash** feature.

SIRI

With the help of Siri, you can perform tasks & receive answers to the questions you ask on your smartwatch. You can tell Siri to translate a phrase, find a place, set an alarm, and more.

Setup Siri

1. On your paired iPhone, navigate to the Settings app, tap on Siri & Search, then activate Listen

for "Hey Siri" and also enable Press Side Button for Siri or Press Home for Siri.

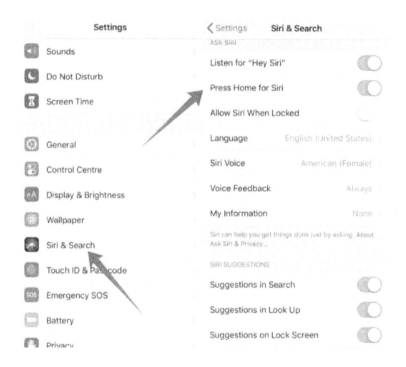

2. On your watch, navigate to the Settings application, click on Siri, then activate the Raise To Speak, Listen for Hey Siri, & Press Digital Crown feature.

How to use Siri

To request for something, carry out any of the below:

❖ Raise your hand and talk to your smartwatch. To deactivate this feature, navigate to the Settings application on your smartwatch, touch Siri, then disable Raise to Speak.
❖ Say "Hey Siri" then say what you want. To disable this feature, navigate to the Settings application, touch Siri, then disable the **Listen for Hey Siri** feature.

❖ Long-press the Digital Crown till the listening indicator appears, and then make a request.
To disable this feature, navigate to the Settings application, touch Siri, and then disable the **Press Digital Crown** feature.

To continue the conversation with Siri, long-press the Digital Crown & start talking

Choose how Siri responds

On your smartwatch, enter the Settings application, touch Siri, touch Siri Response, then select from the below:

❖ Always on: Siri will speak responses, even when you put your device in silent mode.
❖ Control With Silent Mode: Siri's response will be silenced when your smartwatch is set to silent mode.
❖ Headphone only: Siri will only speak response when your smartwatch is connected to Bluetooth headphones.

To change Siri's voice & language, navigate to the Settings application on your smartwatch, touch the **Siri** button, then touch Language or Siri's

Voice. After touching Siri's Voice you can select from the different available voices.

Type to Siri

If you're having trouble speaking, you can write a request to Siri or ask Siri to wait longer for you to finish talking.

* Navigate to the Settings application on your smartwatch
* Head over to Accessibility > Siri and then activate Type to Siri.

❖ If you want Siri to give you more time to finish talking, touch Longer or Longest in the **Siri Pause Time** section

Clear Siri's history

When you make use of Siri, your requests are saved on Apple's servers for 6 months to improve Siri's response to you. You can erase them any time you want.

❖ Navigate to the Settings application on your smartwatch.
❖ Touch the **Siri** button, touch Siri's History, then touch the **Delete Siri History** button.

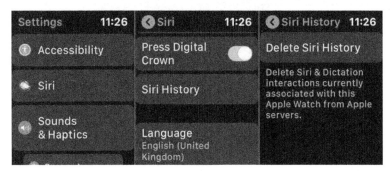

Announce Notifications

Siri can read out notifications from many applications when you are making use of supported Airpods & headphones.

- ❖ Put your earphones on your ear
- ❖ Connect them to your watch.
- ❖ Navigate to the Settings application on your smartwatch.
- ❖ Head over to Siri > Announce Notification, then enable the Announce Notifications feature.

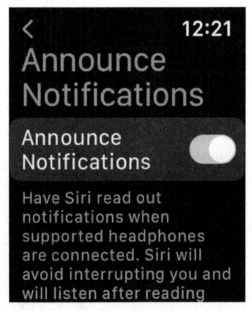

After activating the **Announce Notification** feature, you can select the applications you want audio notifications from by scrolling down and touching every one of them.

Temporarily disable Announce Notifications

❖ Long-press the bottom of your watch display, then swipe up to enter the Control Centre

❖ Tap on the Announce Notification button🔔.

Touch the button🔔 one more time to activate it.

Reply to messages

Say something like, "Reply that is good to know."

Siri will repeat the statement you made, and then request for confirmation before it sends your response. (To send a reply without asking for confirmation, navigate to the Settings application, tap on Siri, click on Announce Notifications, scroll down, and then enable **Reply without Confirmations**.)

Stop Siri from reading a notification

Do any of the below:

❖ Press the Digital Crown.
❖ You could Say "Cancel" or "Stop."

Announce calls with Siri on your smartwatch

The Announce Calls feature allows Siri to identify incoming calls, which you can use your voice to accept or reject.

❖ Navigate to the Settings application on your smartwatch.

❖ Touch the **Siri** button and then enable the **Announce Calls** feature.
❖ When someone calls you, the caller is identified and Siri will ask you if you would like to take the call. You can say "yes" to accept it or "no" to reject it.

APPLE WATCH FACES

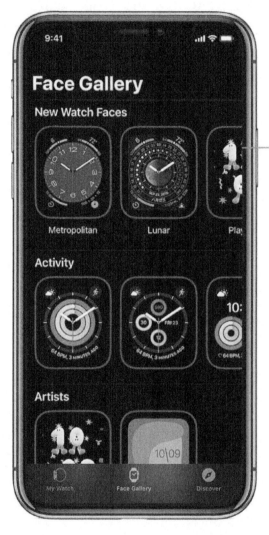

Tap a face to customize it and add it to your collection.

Visit the Apple Watch Face Gallery

You can find all the available watch faces in the Face Gallery in the Watch application on your iPhone. If you find one that you like, you can personalize it, and then add it to your collection.

Open the Face Gallery

Enter the Watch application on your smartphone, and then click on the **Face Gallery** tab in the lower part of your display.

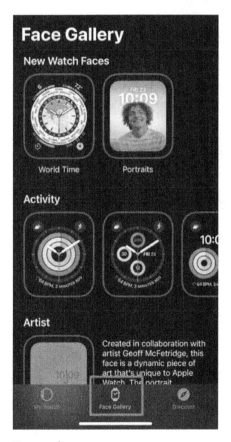

Select features for a watch face

In the Face gallery, touch one of the Faces, then touch any of the features like style or colour.

As you check out different options, the watch face at the upper part of your display changes so that you can see the adjustments you have made to the face.

Add a complication in the Gallery

1. Touch one of the faces in the Face Gallery, then touch any of the complications position, like Bottom Right, Top Right, or Bottom Left.

2. Swipe to view the available complications for that position, then click on any complication you like.

3. If you don't want that position to have a complication, scroll to the beginning of the list and then touch **Off**.

Add a face

❖ After personalizing a watch face in the Face Gallery, click on **Add**.

❖ To use the new watch face on your smartwatch, swipe left across your watch faces till you see the new watch face.

Personalize your watch face

Customize your watch face to look the way you like & provide the features you want. Select one of the designs, change features & colours, then add the watch face to your Face collection.

In the Face Gallery, you will see all the watch faces, personalize the ones you like, and add them to your collection. But if your phone is not with you, you can personalize the watch face on your Apple Watch

Select a different watch face

❖ Swipe across the watch faces to check out the other faces in your collection.
❖ To check out all available watch faces, press & hold the watch face, swipe to the watch face you want to see, and then tap on it.

Swipe left or right to see other watch faces.

Simple

Edit

Add features to your watch face.

Add complications to the watch face

You can add features known as complications to some of your watch faces so that you can instantly check the weather report, prices of stock, etc. from your watch face.

❖ With the watch face showing, press & hold your watch screen, then click on the **Edit** button.
❖ Swipe to the left till you get to the end.

If a watch face has complications, they are displayed on the last screen.

❖ Touch one of the complications to choose it, then rotate the Digital Crown to select another complication—for Instance Home or Heart-Rate.

❖ When you are done, click the Digital Crown to store the changes you have made, then tap on the watch face to move to it.

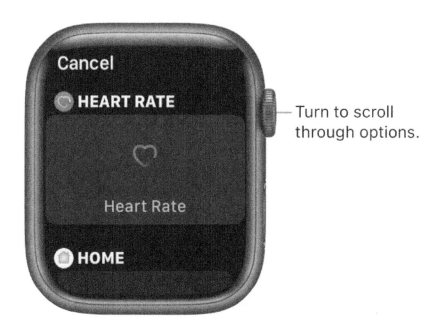

Add a watch face to your collection

You can create a collection of watch faces, even different versions of a design.

❖ With the watch face showing, press & hold your screen.
❖ Swipe left till you get to the end, then click on the Add (+) icon.
❖ Rotate the Digital Crown to view the watch-faces, and then click on the **Add** button.
After adding a watch face, you can now customize it.

Tap new, scroll to browse watch faces, then tap a face to add it.

Check out your face collection

❖ Navigate to the Watch application on your smartphone.

❖ Click on the **My Watch** tab, then swipe through the collection in the **My Faces** segment

You can reorder your watch face collection, by touching **Edit**, then dragging the Rearrange button ≡ beside a watch face down or up.

Delete a watch face from your collection

❖ With a watch face showing, press & hold your watch screen.
❖ Swipe to the watch face you plan on deleting, then swipe the watch face up and click on **Remove**.

Swipe up to delete a watch face, then tap Remove.

Or, launch the Watch application on your smartphone, click on the **My Watch** tab, and then click on **Edit** in the My Faces segment. Click on the Delete button 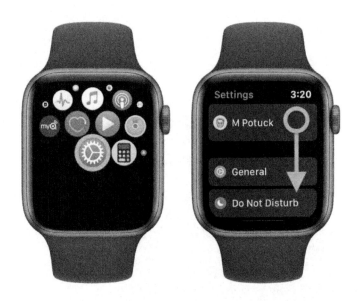 beside the watch face you plan on deleting, then click on the **Remove** button.

Set the watch ahead

❖ Navigate to the Settings application on your smartwatch.

❖ Scroll down, then touch **Clock**.

❖ Click on **+0 min**, and then rotate the Digital Crown to set the watch ahead.

This setting only changes the time displayed on the watch face.

Share Apple Watch faces

❖ Swipe to the watch face you plan on sharing.
❖ Press & hold your watch screen, then click on the Share button 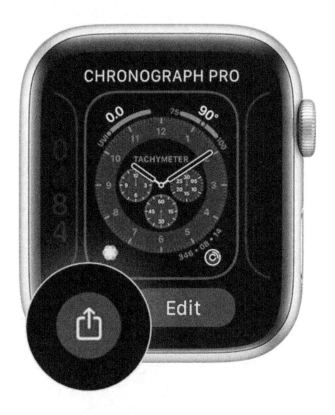.

❖ Tap on the watch face's name, then touch **Don't Include** for a complication that you do not want to share.

❖ Touch one of the recipients, or touch Mail or Message.
If you selected Mail or Message, add a contact, subject & message.

❖ Click on **Send**.

Or, enter the Watch application on your smartphone, touch one of the watch faces from your collection or your Face Gallery, click on the Share button, then select one of the sharing options.

Receive a watch face

You can receive a watch face in the Mail or Message application or by tapping a link.

❖ Open an e-mail, link, or text that has the shared watch face in it.
❖ Touch the shared watch face, and then click on **Add**.

Create a photo watch face

While checking out an image in the Photos application ✷ on your watch, touch the Share button ⬆, scroll down, then click on **Create Face**.

MEASURE YOUR BLOOD OXYGEN LEVEL

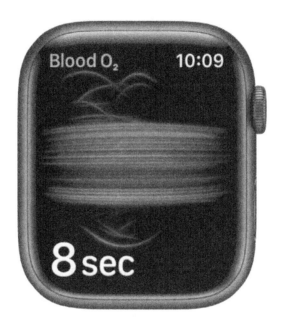

With the Blood Oxygen application, you can measure the amount of oxygen your red blood cells are carrying from your lungs to the other parts of your body. Knowing how much oxygen your blood has can help you understand your overall health & well-being.

Setup Blood Oxygen

- ❖ Navigate to the Settings application.
- ❖ Touch Blood Oxygen, then activate the **Blood Oxygen Measurement** feature.

Disable background measurements when you activate theater mode or Sleep Focus

The blood oxygen meter uses a bright red light that shines on your wrist, making it very visible in dark areas. If the light bothers you, you can deactivate the measurement.

- ❖ Navigate to the Settings application
- ❖ Touch Blood Oxygen, then deactivate In Theater Mode & Sleep Focus

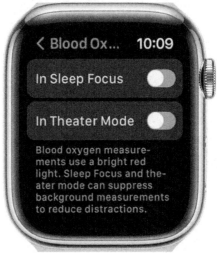

Measuring the level of oxygen in the blood

The Blood Oxygen application can measure your blood oxygen level periodically all through the day if background measurement is enabled, but you can measure it whenever you want.

❖ Navigate to the Blood Oxygen application
❖ Place your hand on a table or on your lap, and ensure your hand is flat and your watch screen is facing up.

❖ Click on the **Start** button, then make sure your arm is still for the next 15 seconds

❖ After the measurement, the results will be displayed on your screen. Touch the **Done** button.

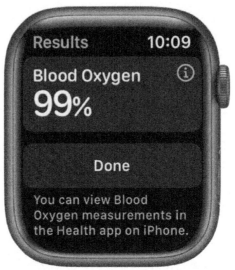

Note: The back of your smartwatch has to be in contact with your skin. Ensure your smartwatch is not loose or very tight on your arm and there should be space for your skin to breath.

Checkout your Blood Oxygen measurement history

❖ Launch the Health application on your phone.
❖ Click on the **Browse** button, touch the **Respiratory** button, then touch the **Blood Oxygen** button.

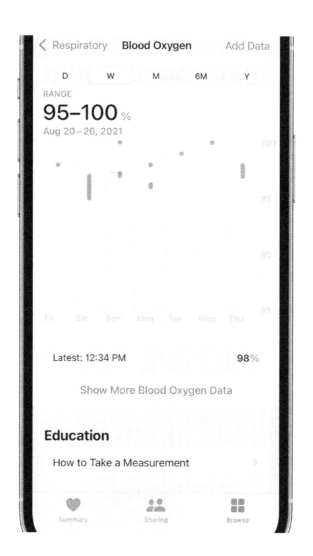

CAMERA REMOTE

If you want to use your iPhone to snap a picture from a distance, you can use your smartwatch to view your phone camera image & capture the picture. You can set the shutter time on your smartwatch to give you enough time to put your wrist down & get ready for the shot.

For this feature to work, your watch & your iPhone has to be within the Bluetooth range (about 10m).

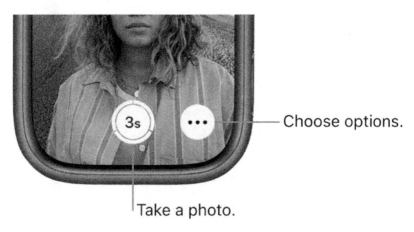

Choose options.

Take a photo.

Take pictures

- ❖ Launch the Camera Remote application on your smartwatch.
- ❖ Set your phone to frame the shot with your smartwatch as the view-finder.
- ❖ Rotate the Digital Crown to zoom
- ❖ To change the exposure, touch the key point of the shot in your smartwatch's preview
- ❖ Touch the Shutter to take the picture

The picture will be stored in the Photos application on your phone but you can review it on your smartwatch.

Review your photos

Use the steps below to review your photos on your smartwatch.

- ❖ Check out a picture: Touch the thumbnail in the lower left corner.
- ❖ Swipe to the left or right to view other pictures.
- ❖ Rotate the Digital Crown to zoom
- ❖ Double tap the picture if you want it to fill your watch screen
- ❖ Touch your screen to display or conceal the Close button & other info

When you are done, touch the **Close** button.

Select another camera & change the settings

❖ Navigate to the Camera Remote application.
❖ Click on the More Options button ● ● ● , then select from any of the options below:
  ➤ Timer
  ➤ Camera (back or front)
  ➤ Flash
  ➤ Live Photo
  ➤ HDR

CYCLE TRACKING

You can record details of your menstrual cycle in the Cycle Tracker application . You can add flow data & symptoms like cramps or headaches. With the info you have recorded, the Cycle Tracking application can predict when your next period or fertile window is about to begin.

Setup Cycle Tracking

❖ Launch the Health application on your iPhone.
❖ Click on the **Browse** button in the bottom right to enter the Health Categories screen.
❖ Touch the **Cycle Tracking** button

❖ Touch the **Get Started** button, then adhere to the guidelines on your display to set notifications & other options.

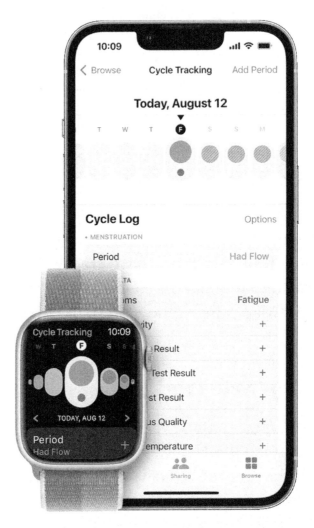

To add or remove options after you've setup Cycle Tracking, launch the Health application on your smartphone, touch the **Browse** button, touch the **Cycle Tracking** button, and then touch Options beside Cycle Log.

Record your cycle on your smartwatch

❖ Launch the Cycle Tracking application on your phone.

❖ Touch the buttons & select options that best describe your period - such as your symptoms.

Your data will appear in the Cycle log on your phone. If you have setup period alerts & Fertility alerts in the Health application on your phone, you'll get notifications on your smartwatch about upcoming fertility windows & periods forecast.

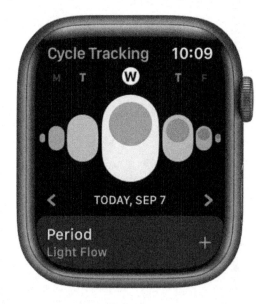

You can also record factors in the Health application that may affect your cycle, like the use of contraceptives, pregnancy, etc.

Important: The Cycle Tracker application shouldn't be used as any type of birth control. Info from this application shouldn't be used to diagnose medical conditions.

MEMOJI

You can create your own Memoji, and select the skin tone, hairstyle, etc. in the Memoji application.

Create a Memoji

❖ Launch the Memoji application.
❖ If this is your first time making use of the Memoji application, click on the **Get Started** button.

If you have used the application before, scroll down, then touch the Add Memoji button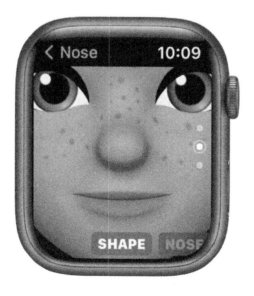 to create another one.

❖ Touch the features you want and rotate the Digital Crown to select your preferred options for the Memoji.

❖ Touch the **Done** button to add the Memoji to the Memoji collection.

To create a new Memoji, click on the Add Memoji button , and add features.

Edit Memoji & more

Launch the Memoji application, touch one of the Memojis, and then select any of the options:

❖ Edit a Memoji: Touch features like headwear & eyes, then rotate the Digital Crown to select one of the variations.
❖ Create a Memoji watch face: Scroll down, then touch the **Create Watch Face** button.
Go back to your Apple watch face, swipe to the left to see the new Memoji watch face.
❖ Touch the **Duplicate** button to duplicate a Memoji
❖ Touch the **Delete** button to delete a Memoji

MINDFULNESS

The Mindfulness application on your smartwatch recommends setting aside a few minutes each day to focus & connect while breathing.

Begin a meditation or breathing session

Navigate to the Mindfulness application, then carry out any of the below:

❖ Reflect: Click on the **Reflect** button, read the topic, focus, and then click on the **Start** button.

❖ Breathe: Touch the **Breath** button, breathe in slowly as the animation increases, breath out as it decreases.

Swipe right to end the session before it completes, then touch the **End** button.

Set the duration of a session

❖ Navigate to the Mindfulness application.
❖ Touch the More Options icon ● ● ● , click on the **Duration** button, and select a duration.

Change mindfulness settings

You can change your reminders, how often you get mindfulness reminders throughout the day, change your breathing rate, & select haptic settings.

Enter the Settings application on your smartwatch, touch Mindfulness, then carry out any of the below:

❖ Set a reminder: In the Reminders section, activate or deactivate Start of the Day & End of the Day; Click on the Add Reminder button to create more reminders.
❖ Receive or disable weekly summary: Enable or disable Weekly Summary.
❖ Silent Reminders: Activate **Mute for Today**.
❖ Change your breathing rate: Touch the **Breathe Rate** button to change the number of breaths per minute.
❖ Select Haptics settings: Touch the **Haptic** button, then select Prominent, Minimal, or None.
❖ Get new meditations: Activate the **Add New Meditations to Watch** feature to download new reflections when your device is charging.

You can also enter the Watch application on your phone, touch the **My Watch** tab, touch the Mindfulness button, and then change any of the settings.

Use the breath watch face

Add the Breath watch face for fast access to a mindfulness session.

* ❖ Long-press the current watch face.
* ❖ Swipe to the left till you get to the end, then touch the Add (+) button.
* ❖ Rotate the Digital Crown to choose Breath, then touch the **Add** button
* ❖ Touch the watch face to launch the Mindfulness application.

APPLE PAY

Apple Pay offers an easy and safe way to make payments on your smartwatch.

Add a card to your smartwatch with your phone

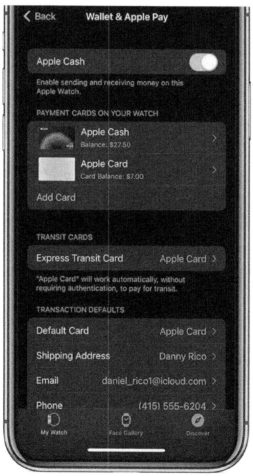

- ❖ Navigate to the Watch application on your smartphone.
- ❖ Click on the **My Watch** button, then click on the **Wallet and Apple Pay** button
- ❖ Touch the **Add Card** button, and then adhere to the guidelines on your display.

Your card issuer may ask for more steps to verify your info.

Add a card on your smartwatch

You can add transit, debit, & credit cards right on your watch.

- ❖ Navigate to the Wallet application on your smartwatch.
- ❖ Scroll down, and then click on **Add Cards**.
- ❖ Select Transit Card, Credit or Debit Card, or Apple Account; and then adhere to the guidelines on your display.

Select your default card

- ❖ Launch the Watch application on your smartphone.

- ❖ Click on the **My Watch** button, click on Wallet and Apple Pay, click on Default card, and then choose any of your cards.

Rearrange your payment cards

Navigate to the Wallet application on your watch, press & hold one of the cards, then drag the card to another position.

Remove a card

- ❖ Navigate to the Wallet application on your watch.
- ❖ Touch to select one of the cards
- ❖ Scroll down, and then click on **Remove**.

You can also enter the Watch application on your iPhone, touch the **My Watch** tab, touch the **Wallet and Apple Pay** button, touch the card, then touch the **Remove Card** button

Change your default transaction information

You can change transaction info—including e-mail, default card, shipping address, etc.

* ❖ Navigate to the Watch application on your smartphone.
* ❖ Click on the **My Watch** button, click on Wallet and Apple Pay, then scroll down to display Transaction Defaults.
* ❖ Touch one of the items to edit it.

Pay for items in a store with your smartwatch

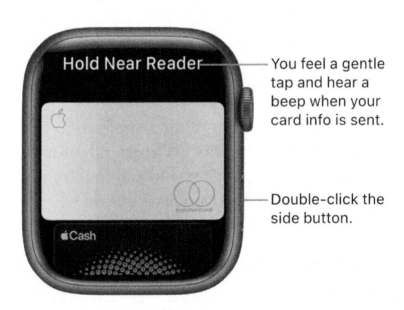

* ❖ Press the side button two times quickly.

- ❖ Scroll to select one of the cards.
- ❖ Take your smartwatch very close to the contactless card reader, and ensure your watch screen is facing the reader.

You'll feel a tap & hear a beep when the payment detail has been sent.

You'll get a notification in the Notifications Center when the transaction has been confirmed.

Pay for items in an application

- ❖ When shopping in an app on your smartwatch, select the Apple Pay option when checking out.
- ❖ Go through your billing & shipping info, then press the side button two times quickly to pay for the item with your watch.

WORKOUT

The Workout application gives you tools to manage each workout. You can set goals like calories, distance, & time. Your smartwatch will track your progress, nudge you along the way, & summarize your results.

Start a workout

Tap to set workout goals.

Turn the Digital Crown to choose another workout.

- Launch the Workout application.
- Rotate the Digital Crown to go to one of the available workouts.
  For workouts like surfing or kickboxing, touch the **Add Workout** button in the lower part of your display.
- When you are ready to start, touch the Workout.

Adjust your watch while working out

While working out, you can:

- See your progress: Raise your hand to view your workout stats. Rotate the Digital Crown to see other workout options like Elevation, Power, & Segment.
- Pause & resume a workout: To pause a workout, press the Digital Crown & the side button simultaneously. You can also swipe to the right on a workout screen, and then touch the **Pause** button. Touch the **Resume** button to continue the workout.

❖ Rock out while working out: While working out, swipe to the left to the Now Playing screen to select songs & control your Bluetooth headphones volume. To select a playlist that will automatically start playing when you start a workout, enter the Watch application on your phone, then touch the **My Watch** tab. Touch the **Workout** button, click on Workout Playlist, and select a playlist.

End the workout

After reaching your goal, you will hear a sound & feel a vibration. If you're fine and want to continue, go ahead — your smartwatch will continue to collect data till you tell it to stop. When you want to end the workout:

❖ Swipe to the right, then touch the **End** button.

❖ Rotate the Digital Crown to go through the summary of the results, then touch the **Done** button in the lower part of your display.

Review your workout history

❖ Enter the Fitness application on your phone.
❖ Click on the **Summary** button, then touch one of the workouts

Start a swimming workout

❖ Navigate to the Workout application.
❖ Select the **Pool Swim** or the **Open Water Swim** option.

Press the Digital Crown & the side button simultaneously to pause the workout.

When you begin a swimming workout, your smartwatch will automatically lock its screen to prevent accidental taps. When you are done with the workout, long-press the Digital Crown to unlock your watch display & remove the water from the speakers. You will hear a sound & feel water around your hand.

Manually clear water after swimming

❖ Long-press the lower part of your display, swipe up to reveal the Controls Centre, then touch the Water Lock button 💧.
❖ Long-press the Digital Crown to unlock your watch display & remove the water from the speakers.

Use gym equipment with your Apple Watch

Your smartwatch can pair & synchronize data with compatible cardio equipment like indoor bikes, treadmills, etc., giving you accurate workout info.

To connect your smartwatch to the gym equipment, adhere to the directives below:

❖ Check if the device is compatible - you will see "Connect to Apple Watch" on the device.
❖ Ensure your smartwatch is set to detect fitness devices—enter the Settings application on your

smartwatch, touch the **Workout** button, and then activate the **Detect Gym Equipment** feature.

❖ Take your smartwatch very close to the contactless reader on the equipment, and ensure the screen is facing the reader.
You'll feel a soft tap & hear a beep when your smartwatch pairs with the gym equipment.

If the Detect Gym Equipment feature is disabled on your smartwatch, navigate to the Workout application, then take your smartwatch very close to the contactless reader on the equipment, and ensure your watch screen is facing the reader.

Start & end a workout

Press the **Start** button on the equipment to start the workout. Press the **Stop** button on the equipment when you're done.

After ending a workout, the data from the equipment will appear in the workout summary in the Activity application on your smartwatch & the Fitness application on your phone.

Automatically pause cycling & running workouts

❖ Navigate to the Settings application on your smartwatch.
❖ Touch the **Workout** button, then activate the **Auto-Pause** feature

Your smartwatch will automatically pause & resume your cycling & outdoor running workouts, for instance, if you stop to drink water. You can press the Digital Crown & the side button simultaneously to pause the workout manually.

Activate or deactivate workout reminders

If your smartwatch senses that you are swimming, running, or doing other exercises it will alert you to start the Workout application. Adhere to the directives below to activate or deactivate this feature.

❖ Enter the Settings application on your smartwatch.

❖ Touch the **Workout** button, then change the Start Workout Reminders & End Workout Reminders setting.

Save power while working out

You can extend your watch battery while exercising.

❖ Enter the Settings application on your smartwatch.
❖ Touch the **Workout** button, and then activate the **Low Power Mode** feature.

INDEX

swimming, 11, 153, 156

T

Text Size, 53
Theater Mode, 51, 125
time, 5, 11, 17, 44, 45, 55, 56, 73, 75, 76, 85, 96, 104, 106, 121, 129, 137, 149

U

unlock, 4, 28, 69, 70, 71, 153
update, 6, 10, 82

V

volume, 5, 6, 54, 66, 151

W

watch face, 7, 8, 9, 10, 9, 13, 22, 35, 38, 45, 46, 47, 58, 59, 85, 111, 112, 113, 114, 115, 116, 117, 118, 119, 121, 122, 123, 139, 143
Wifi, 64, 78, 93
Workout, 149, 150, 151, 153, 155, 156, 157

Printed in Great Britain
by Amazon

23442119R00096